SOBER and PISSED OFF

Jane Zarse

To my all-loving, all-inclusive God

"If we were to live, we had to be free of anger. The grouch and the brainstorm were not for us. They may be the dubious luxury of normal men, but for alcoholics these things are poison."

Alcoholics Anonymous, p. 66

Preface

There are a lot of sober and pissed off members of Alcoholics Anonymous. I have sat in thousands of AA meetings listening to them complain about people and circumstances that are out of their control. Meetings are a great outlet for us where we can talk about everything and drink about nothing. There are many members who are not drinking, but they're also not happy.

I like to bounce around to different meetings, as there is a danger of inbred thinking when we only attend the same meeting with the same people. It gets to the point where I'll already know what people are going to say or what story they are going to tell based on the topic. Even though I was attending different meetings, I was noticing reoccurring themes. I was hearing a lot of ungrateful alcoholics. I would go weeks without being able to avoid hearing a member getting all bent out of shape over road rage or some other uncontrollable situation.

Just as there are different levels of alcoholism, there are different levels of recovery. The difference between physical sobriety and emotional sobriety is the difference between chicken shit and chicken salad. I know what it's like to be emotionally sober, feeling happy, joyous, and free. I also know what it's like to be dry and pissed off. I was such a low-bottom drunk that once I became physically sober, I felt so grateful to be alive that I was on a pink cloud for years. I would thank God every morning when I opened my eyes for another day of sobriety. I was experiencing peace in my heart by walking in love and trusting God with every fiber of my being. After a few years, however, I started taking my sobriety for granted. I was depending less on God and more on myself. I allowed my ego to have more control and became increasingly unhappy. It got to the point where I was feeling anger first thing in the morning instead of love. I wasn't drinking, but I was attending fewer meetings. I was disappointed and horrified to discover that I too had become a dry and miserable alcoholic. Something had to change, because I was scared I would end up drinking again. I believed in the power of God and the program to grant me physical sobriety, and now I needed to let them help me achieve emotional wellbeing too.

1

I had my last drink on September 14, 2009. However, I count September 15, 2009 as my sobriety date because it was such a rarity that I'd made it an entire twenty-four hours without a drink. I'm still in awe of my sobriety. I'd been attending AA meetings for over a year and drinking the entire time. I refused to accept that I was powerless over alcohol and was only attending meetings hoping to learn how to drink without horrible consequences. Alcohol was my relief for emotional and mental torment. It was my unchallenged solution for everything, and it dictated my daily life for years.

Alcoholics move at the speed of pain, and we can take a lot of it as long as it allows us to keep drinking. It's amazing what we will put ourselves through to keep feeding the beast. I was abusing my body with an obscene amount of alcohol every day. I was so physically dependent that I believed I was drinking to live. I was living in a state of denial. I hated myself and my life. I was physically, mentally, spiritually, and financially spent. I didn't have the guts to kill myself, so I was methodically drinking myself to death. I was slowly committing suicide on the installment plan. You can't scare an alcoholic. I knew I was dying, and the goal was to stay drunk enough not to care.

My relationship with alcohol started off quite innocently. I started drinking socially with my friends in high school and thought it was magic. I loved the way it made me feel. It made me feel prettier, funnier, a better dancer, fill in the blank. I thought I'd found a magic potion to carry me through life. It would give me a false sense of security and make me feel more comfortable in my skin. What makes me an alcoholic is that what alcohol did *for* me trumped what alcohol did *to* me. I went through the three stages of social drinking, trouble drinking, and merry-go-round drinking. I knew it was killing me, but I cared more about the relief of temporary escapism than I did about saving my own life.

When it comes to alcoholism, I am the real deal. I was born in Lake Forest, Illinois and raised in the private school world of privilege and excess. My father was a full member of the Chicago Board of Trade. We resided in a ninety-two-hundred-square-foot lakefront estate, and I graduated from Boston University on the Dean's List. But alcohol is the great remover; it will take everything you care about before it goes in for the physical kill. In my last year of drinking, I was an acute alcoholic sleeping on a couch in Gary, Indiana. I was penniless, unemployable, and borderline for alcohol-induced dementia. My daughter was just shy of two years old and was living at my father's winter house on Boca Grande, a small residential community on Gasparilla Island in southwest Florida. It is very difficult for a mother to admit that her child is better off in other hands, but I knew it was true. I was so far down the scale that I could admit I was an unfit parent. I wasn't even living. I was barely existing, at best.

2

I never wanted to get sober for me. Quite frankly, I didn't think I was worth it. I was blessed with a graceful dry spell during my pregnancy, because I was willing to change my alcohol consumption for the sake of my unborn child, whom I felt was worth the effort. As soon as she was born, my baby was on the bottle and so was Mommy. My alcoholism made me feel worthless, helpless, and hopeless every day. If it wasn't for my blameless, beautiful child, I probably would have died of my disease. My love for my daughter was the only thing that made me entertain joining Alcoholics Anonymous. Rebellious alcoholic personalities die hard. I thought attending these meetings would sober me up. I had no idea how much work this would actually entail.

When I first started attending AA meetings, I saw the word "God" on the wall and found it daunting. I thought, *I just want to quit drinking, not be bombarded by a bunch of holy rollers.* I also thought everyone was full of shit. In my mind, they were either not a real alcoholic like me, or they were also drinking outside of meetings. I thought it was impossible for anyone with my compulsion to abstain from alcohol for any substantial amount of time. I thought I was terminally unique, and I had no intention of following their directions. I was treating AA like Burger King and hoping to achieve sobriety by ordering the program my way. I would show up sporadically and expect my relationship with alcohol to improve. In essence, I was not done.

My mental health was already long gone, and my physical health was starting to follow. My kidneys were beginning to shut down, and I was in and out of the emergency room for Ativan drips because of my chronic, violent detoxing. I would drink myself into oblivion every night, just to awaken to the Four Horsemen terror, bewilderment, frustration, and despair that each morning brought. My life felt like the movie *Groundhog Day* (The Alcoholic Torture Edition). I had to concede that my way was not working. I knew that if I wanted to be sober, I had to surrender my will and my way.

I started cutting down my consumption, trying to detox myself. Quitting cold turkey was simply not an option. I can resentfully recall ex-husbands and old boyfriends trying to cut me off completely. They wouldn't even allow me one fucking beer, in an attempt to "help me." The second they were no longer looking, I would guzzle anything I could get my hands on. Detox for an acute alcoholic is extremely dangerous and should be assisted medically.

Even though I didn't get sober my first year in Alcoholics Anonymous, my perception of God and the members began to change. I could not deny that people were living very rewarding lives that were free from alcohol. This gave me hope that maybe, just maybe, that could be me too. Hope for an alcoholic is a really big deal. It means believing that good things can happen when everything looks bleak. The members credited God or a higher power with their newfound freedom and happiness. I'd always believed in God, but I was convinced that God didn't believe in me because of all my failures and mistakes. The solution in AA is spiritual, not logical, however. I had two choices: (1) keep drinking myself to death, or (2) accept spiritual help. There was no door number three. Faced with this fatal nature, I became as open-minded and willing as only the dying can be.

Starting over in recovery means we can also start over in our spiritual life. I needed to find a power greater than alcohol to preclude me from drinking myself to death. I now choose to call that power God. Like many people, I believe that God brought me to AA and AA brought me to God. If you find the word "God" off-putting, you can choose another term. A lot of people feel more comfortable using the term "Higher Power" (HP). Other common alternatives include "Love," "the Universe," "my Creator," and "my Beloved." I personally don't believe what we call God matters. I do believe the love of God can renew anyone's mind, body, and spirit. God loves you and is available to you, and all you need to do is believe. Belief is the only metric that really matters. I have lived this amazing grace firsthand.

Alcoholics are defiant by nature, and I am no exception. Tell me not to do something, and I want to do it twice and take pictures. King Alcohol had beaten me into submission, though, and I had to admit defeat. This admission was the first step in rebuilding my life. I was not willing to give up one more thing for my drinking, and I was willing to do whatever it took to stay sober. This meant surrendering to the simple program of Alcoholics Anonymous and thoroughly following its path. I found a sponsor, got into the literature, worked the steps, and believed in a Higher Power. I was working the program, and the program was working for me. It turns out I wasn't so unique after all.

I learned that alcoholism is a twofold problem: a mental obsession coupled with a physical allergy. I had a mind that was obsessed with alcohol and a body that was allergic to it, meaning that when I drink, I experience the phenomenon of craving, leaving my body always screaming for more.

I also learned that I had a thinking problem and my drinking was just a symptom. I used to have a self-defeating mind. A concrete example of this is that I never thought I could quit drinking—and with that mindset, I was 100% correct. When I believed God could relieve me of my alcoholism, He did. We become what we think and will never go beyond what we believe. My negative thinking resulted in a miserable existence and nearly killed me.

I hid out in AA because I didn't trust myself. I was attending two or three meetings a day. I didn't just need to quit drinking; I needed to learn how to live without alcohol. I needed to build the new, not just get rid of the old. I couldn't fix my destructive thinking on my own. While listening to other members, I was learning new thinking patterns and coping skills. It also felt good to be around other people after living in isolation for years. King Alcohol had convinced me that I didn't need other people. My theme song used to be Men at Work's "Who Can It Be Now?" I was a maladjusted loner. It felt so good to be surrounded by people who seemed genuinely happy to see me after my drinking had ostracized me from family and friends. I was experiencing kindness and encouragement. It meant the world to me when someone would tell me it was nice to see me. It gave me inspiration and a drive to keep getting better. I had been miserable long enough and was ready for a change.

The biggest lie alcohol told me was, "You are not enough." I didn't just need to come to terms with my sobriety; I needed to accept my humanity. I was a perfectionist who didn't have what it took to keep up, so I gave up. I didn't feel good enough, so I simply stopped trying. Alcohol broke my spirit long before it started destroying my mind and body. The chronic drinking made me feel worthless and useless. It's impossible to feel good about yourself when you are reaching for a bottle every morning. Self-loathing was an unpleasant surprise that I never saw coming. It felt like a pit in my stomach filled with shame, heartbreak, and disappointment. Alcohol exacerbated these feelings. I felt like disappointment personified. When I was drinking, my feelings felt infinite and eternal. I had no hope for personal improvement. I saw no way out, so I continued to isolate and drink to deal with my pain.

My self-esteem was already compromised when I first started exhibiting signs of acute alcoholism. It started physically with high anxiety, hand tremors, and chest pain. I chalked it up to stress and anxiety and used it as another reason why I needed to drink. I never wanted to admit that I was experiencing chronic daily detox. This discomfort was the beginning of my now-justified morning drinking. I needed a few pops to steady my hands, calm myself, and feel "normal." As a drunk, I learned to ignore the pointing and whispers when I was out publicly and over-served. This new, physical demand was impossible to ignore. This imperative need to have a constant stream of booze in my system made me feel defective. I tried to hide my newfound condition by drinking alone before I would meet others out for drinks. My hands were difficult to control and would shake violently. Signing my name or getting a manicure was extremely problematic without a sufficient amount of booze in my system. Additionally, I didn't sleep. I would have to drink enough to pass out. I ignored what alcohol was doing to me and just learned to live with these new handicaps. I lived like this for well over ten years.

I never imagined I would grow up to be a full-blown alcoholic. I thought I was far too smart and privileged to waste my life dicking around with addiction. I remember when I was a freshman at Boston University, Kitty Dukakis was hospitalized for drinking rubbing alcohol. At the time, I thought, *How could anybody be so desperate and stupid*? Twenty years later, a woman in a meeting described how she also drank alcohol out of the medicine cabinet because she so desperately "needed" a drink. She felt her body demand it, and I could completely relate. I also had the same judgmental, preconceived notions about alcoholics that many people do. I thought it was a lack of willpower or low moral character. I never imagined that I would give my life away for a substance, but that's exactly what happened. King Alcohol was the master and I was the slave. My alcoholism was all-encompassing, and every aspect of my life revolved around my drinking.

3

When I finally managed to put the plug in the jug, I started to regain my life. I felt so proud of putting the drink down and racking up some sober time. I felt like I was finally regaining the control I so desperately craved. I was well aware that my sobriety was not of my own doing. Rather, I credited God and AA for keeping me sober. I no longer felt alone. I believe in an all-loving, all-inclusive God who is constantly with me and interested in every detail of my life. As a drunk, I was tortured by loneliness. In sobriety, I found a loving God and a supportive network of friends. The main part of the battle is getting in the right frame of mind. God and the loving members of AA gave me this gift. I couldn't fix my wacky thinking on my own. I was ill-equipped for that task. Through God and AA, though, I was learning to appreciate the ordinary, and this made my life extraordinary. When I started to act like life was a blessing, it began to feel like one.

Drinking cut me off from God. Regardless of one's religious background or belief system, destructive drinking builds a barrier between ourselves and God. My drinking also cut me off from other people. As a drunk, I lived without any real companionship. Alcohol became my only friend, and I became comfortable in isolation. I stopped answering my phone and opening my mail. I would even use the back entrance of many different apartment buildings throughout the years to avoid exchanging pleasantries with the doormen. The loneliness is one of the worst things about drinking, and the supportive fellowship of AA is a delightful release from feeling all alone. It is commonly stated that AA members have paid the highest initiation fee of any club in the world. We have paid with terrible physical punishments and remorseful mental anguish, not to mention all the money wasted on liquor. With God's love and the gift of bonding with other members, nothing feels so painful or insurmountable now that I feel compelled to drink over it.

I finally felt like I could be myself in the rooms of AA—whoever that was. After spending wasted years inebriated, I was still trying to figure out who I was. I trusted these people enough to be honest about my destructive drinking and pathetic circumstances. They told me that we are as sick as our secrets, so I tossed all of my bullshit and false bravado out the window. I knew I had to be rigorously honest to be sober, so early on, I began treating AA like an emotional nudist colony. I'd finally found my people. There is safety in numbers for alcoholics like me, men and women united against a common fatal disease. I let these people see me stripped down to the bone. I abandoned my ego, my fear of other people and their opinions, and my painful obsession with self. I got drunk, but we stayed sober. Our common welfare comes first. I know that AA would be perfectly fine without me, but I don't have a snowball's chance in hell of making it without AA.

I hated when AA members would tell me, "You are exactly where you are supposed to be." I would grin and think, "Uh, no, I grew up rich and privileged, and I wasn't supposed to end up this way." It was like my life was the result of some sort of clerical error and I needed to speak to the manger. This bullshit attitude kept me drunk. Refusing to acknowledge my pain didn't make it go away. Denial is a protective device—it protects the pain and makes it stronger. I refused to acknowledge realities that would hurt my feelings. My self-centered drinking distorted my perception and made it difficult to let go of expectations and accept my reality as it was. By the end of my drinking, I was losing touch with reality. I can recall falling off barstools thinking I had it going on. I was running on fumes and ego.

When I came to realize that I was powerless over alcohol, surrender was my only option. I was done wrestling with King Alcohol, because I never won a match. It was a fixed fight. The back and forth of wanting to drink and not wanting to drink was finally over. In surrender, I finally found freedom. The gift of understanding finally reached me, and I knew I couldn't drink anymore. I'd lived in alcoholic torture for most of my adult life. I'd never thought I would be able to quit drinking because of the relentless mental obsession for a drink to calm my inner conflict. When mentally obsessed, alcohol overshadows everything else. The biggest gift by far that I have received from AA was losing the mental obsession with alcohol. I'd never even seen the point of quitting drinking if I was still going to be thinking about it. I don't know how it left or precisely when. All I know is, as promised, it was long gone. It's really easy not to drink if you're not even thinking about it. If I was still obsessed with alcohol, I would have picked it back up years ago and probably would have drank myself to death by now. Most women who drank like me died of the disease. I'm extremely grateful not to have ended up another statistic.

4

With my newfound sobriety and freedom, I was also told I could reinvent myself. This was great news! I was so sick of myself and my drunken existence. I was an unemployable, unfit parent sleeping on a couch in Gary, Indiana. I stayed drunk because I couldn't stand myself or my life. Before AA, my drinking had made me unpredictable and unreliable, and I wanted to be a credible person of substance. I was done with the false promises and harmful habits of drunken insanity. This admission of weakness becomes a source of strength in rebuilding a new life. I was told, "Stick with the winners."

There are obviously good examples and bad examples in AA. I did not want to be a chronic relapser, but I hate it when people say relapse is not a part of recovery. It makes them sound like they've never read The Big Book of Alcoholics Anonymous. Relapse is mentioned many times in the book, and it is part of many people's recovery. It took me over a year to finally put the drink down because I'd finally reached a place of grim determination with no reservations.

I surrounded myself with winners who had many years of uninterrupted sobriety under their belt. I wanted what they had. There is an unspoken hierarchy in the rooms, though it's said that we're all just one drink away from a drunk. I agree that just one drink is the kiss of death for an alcoholic, but I don't think the alcoholic with 20 hours sober is in the same league as the alcoholic with 20 years sober.

I had to remember that I was addicted to a legal substance and needed to learn to behave accordingly. I got lucky in the sense that I got sober in a house full of liquor. Because I was couch-surfing and unable to maintain my own residence, I still lived with friends who drank. We are told in AA to play the tape all the way through if we ever feel like picking up. In early sobriety, I got to watch the live show. I would watch as my friends would start drinking with ease and comfort, and by the end of the night, I would watch them morph into disoriented, angry drunks. I was not jealous and didn't feel like I was missing out on anything. Many people treat recovering alcoholics like we still *want* to drink but we just white-knuckle it. They think we are hungry cartoon characters with big eyes and alcohol is the raw steak that we are salivating over. This could not be further from the truth. I want to stay sober more than I want to drink. I am indifferent to alcohol— safe and protected. Now that I am living in the solution, the problem has been removed. I can go anywhere neither cocky nor afraid.

I was starting to feel alive, happy, and grateful as I began to live a sober life. Alcohol had robbed me of these feelings, and it felt miraculous that I was living and loving life free from alcohol. AA is not a theory. It is a life of sober, normal living. In recovery from my self-imposed crisis, I was asked to decide whether God is everything or nothing. God either is or He isn't. I knew that for me, God is absolutely everything. I had always believed in God, and now I could feel and see Him working in my life. No human power could have relieved my alcoholism. There is no known cure for alcoholism. The only proven treatment is a spiritual one. Due to a divine intervention, I am living a new life free from alcohol. I have exchanged a life of drunkenness, failure, and defeat for a life of sobriety, peace of mind, and usefulness. I hold my life in trust for God.

When I quit drinking, my brain was pretty fried. Now that I was sober, I wanted and needed to take care of myself, but I really didn't know how. I went to multiple AA meetings a day because I needed a lot of help. I had no experience being sober, and I needed to learn how to live life on life's terms without escaping reality. I was told, "Keep bringing the body, and the mind will follow." I am one of the lucky ones who really enjoys attending meetings. Even in the beginning, I felt so fortunate to have these meetings to help me cope with and talk about my alcoholism. I'd been alone with this disease for a very long time, and finding other people committed to freedom from alcohol was a godsend. Just being open and honest about my drunken isolation was extremely therapeutic. I loved listening to the other members and hung on every word. I was experiencing something new. I didn't feel the need to have to explain myself. In the outside world, I never felt completely comfortable, but in AA, for the first time, I could just *be*.

I was also able to talk about my embarrassing life circumstances created by addiction. As a drunk, I'd been so ashamed of being sick and poor. I drove around in an old car with a cracked windshield that I couldn't afford to fix. I looked horrible and I didn't even bother to care. My wardrobe had dwindled down to two pairs of pants from Fashion Bug, one bra, and a few tops. When you are living with friends and have no home, personal possessions fall by the wayside. I carried around an old Louis Vuitton bag with a broken zipper (secretly hoping nobody noticed). I wore old, scuffed boots and a solid gold Rolex from Harrods. When the fog lifted, I was actually able to laugh at myself. I could laugh at the absurdity of my addiction.

Yes, I was laughing again. I would both laugh and cry at the tables, and it felt great to be alive. Keeping a sense of humor about circumstances that would have typically overwhelmed me made things seem more bearable. I was getting better, and I was having a good time doing it. The AA crowd is not a glum lot. We are people who tried to escape pain unsuccessfully, and we need each other to heal our pain collectively. We cannot stay sober alone. Laughter usually erupts over shared experiences that bond us. These experiences are often humiliating. I would laugh when members would talk about digging through couch cushions for change to buy a bottle, because I did that too. I was learning how to live in recovery, and that included learning how to have fun again.

I was becoming comfortable in my own skin. I was reclaiming my self-esteem by doing esteemable acts. I wasn't drinking, I was honest, and I was always doing the next-right thing. I was learning new spiritual principles such as hope, faith, and perseverance, and then applying them to my daily life. My mind stopped racing, and I was learning how to enjoy the moment. Sobriety allowed me to be a participant in my own life. I was working hard on becoming the mother that my daughter deserved, and I took this task very seriously. I was still poor, sick, and confused, but I was starting to feel good about myself. Happiness is the byproduct of living right. I now had the courage to face painful and difficult situations head-on. I was done with hiding and escaping. This courageous perseverance was gifted to me through my Higher Power. I know that God works for me and through me. I am certain that God continues to do for me what I could not do for myself. When I fell in love with God and AA, I knew I was going to be okay.

5

The love of my daughter is what brought me into AA. It is commonly said that we need to get sober for ourselves, but that isn't always the case. People come to their first meeting for a variety of reasons: the loss of a job, a marriage, or a driver's license. I've never seen anyone show up on a winning streak. For the members who lost their children, there is a special kind of urgency. My daughter was living with my father because my drinking had made me an unfit mother. I wanted to change so I could be a good mother for my only child. I met many other women who had reconnected with their children in recovery. Their happy endings gave me hope and strength. I would drive around listening to "The Reason" by Hoobastank, hell-bent on becoming a woman my daughter could be proud of.

I didn't just make a firm decision to quit drinking; I was slowly becoming the person I should have been a long time ago. I had love and good intentions in my heart, and the universe was rewarding my positive changes. We create our own reality. Having changed my thinking, I was now living in a universe that supported me. This felt a lot different than the world that I'd thought was against me. The world was not the problem; I was. After abandoning my victim mentality and taking accountability, I could see what needed to be changed in me and my attitudes. True spirituality is knowing that no matter what, everything is already okay. If I don't drink, I get to stay in the game and will always have a chance. For this alcoholic, one drink would mean game over.

My daughter came to live with me when I had one year and one week of sobriety. I was out of the woods and felt secure in my program. I needed to feel safe and secure before I could provide that for my child. In active alcoholism, I never felt secure because I was never safe from self-destruction. I can recall attending three AA meetings in one day and buying a bottle of vodka on the way home. Many times, it felt like my car would go on autopilot and pull into bars or liquor stores on the way home. It's baffling when you find yourself drinking after you swore off the stuff, but it happens. I would share this at meetings, and some members wrote me off as a lost cause. The funny thing about AA is that it is not horse racing, so we really shouldn't be taking bets on who we think is going to make it. The winners just might surprise us.

When I got my one-year coin, it felt bittersweet. As a drunk, I'd always dreamt that if I quit drinking I would be exceptionally successful. This just wasn't the case. I collected my coin and felt like I should have been further along financially. I even felt a little disappointed in myself. This was quickly overshadowed by knowing that I was going to be imminently reunited with my daughter. Though I still didn't have the wherewithal to sustain my own residence, I was living with a long-haul truck driver from the program. I would watch the house and his little dog while he was on the road. It was a protected environment, and I was living rent-free. I was thrilled to have my daughter back in my life.

Good things happen to drunks who don't drink. My daughter, Paige, was three years old at the time and had no recollection of seeing me drunk, and I am intent on keeping it this way.

The reconnection with my daughter felt completely natural. I was confident that I could be the mother she needed. I would cringe for the drunken days when I would drop her off at daycare and know that she was in better hands. You know you are an unfit parent when you think your child is in more capable hands with a stranger. Alcohol stole my humanity. She was so loving toward me, it took a lot of meetings and internal work not to feel so undeserving of her love. It was still new for me to actually allow myself to feel love from another human being, even my only child. All I wanted to do was be in her presence, so I barely worked and didn't send her to daycare for over six months. I was finally enjoying living in the present moment without any thoughts of the past or future. I was spending quality time with my daughter and didn't want to be anywhere else. We would play with dolls and go to the park. I would take her to Dollar Tree and tell her I would buy her anything in the store. We were really having fun. These were the days I'd been waiting and working for, and I was consciously aware of how blessed I was.

My addiction also did a number on my credit report. It's really difficult to pay bills when you don't open the mail and have no source of income. If a creditor got me on the phone, I would tell him that I would put his number in a hat and get back to him if he was the lucky winner. In active alcoholism, I went into survival mode. I lived to continue drinking, void of any real emotions or comprehensive thinking. I'm not quite sure how, but I always found money for booze and even had a dollar to put in the AA basket. However, I didn't pay my bills for years, and the consequences were going to be with me for a while. The first thing I learned about having bad credit is that I was no longer in a position to call the shots. A bad credit score ensures you will usually pay more for less product. When I went to buy a used car, my credit score dictated which car I would drive and how much I would pay. They literally told me which car they were willing to sell me.

They told me I could have a used Chevy Cobalt with manual, wind-down windows for $330 a month. Sold! The truth is, I was grateful to have it and didn't really care about the padded bill. I just chalked it up as more collateral damage from my drinking.

6

     I was really enjoying my sobriety. I was running, reading, and spending quality time with my daughter. I was busy collecting moments, not things. Life felt like the John Lennon song "Watching the Wheels" every single day, and my heart was full and content. I had little money and had never been happier, but it was time to go to work.

     Paige started preschool, and I went to work in earnest. I trusted God, remained disciplined, and my job really started to take off. I was able to lease my own apartment for myself and my daughter. When I drove to pick up the keys to my own residence, after being effectively homeless for years, tears of gratitude streamed down my face. This was my dream. Having my own place for myself and my daughter was the goal, and here it was, coming to fruition. I was over the moon.

I was on a pink cloud. I thanked God first thing every morning when I opened my eyes. I really believe we need to get squared away spiritually before tangible blessings start showing up. Being responsible, being a good mother, making my own money, and paying my bills on time built up my self-esteem. I was actually proud of myself. I was living a life way better than anything I'd ever imagined. As a drunk, I'd really just wanted the pain to stop. I'd never envisioned life could get this good. I became bolder in my prayers. I prayed for a successful business, and God delivered like Domino's. I became a business owner with hundreds of clients and a residual income stream for years to come. I put my trust in God, and His grace far exceeded anything I could have planned.

AA also gave me the most ideal social life. I could have as much of it or as little as I wanted. There was always something to do. When members tell a newcomer, "You never have to be alone again," they mean it. All holidays and special occasions are covered, and nobody ever feels left out. This is a really big deal to many of us who have felt ostracized by friends and family. I went to many of these events to practice socializing without drinking. It's funny, but I had no experience socializing without booze. In the past, I wouldn't even entertain going to events without alcohol and didn't trust anyone who didn't drink. I could work any room with ease while holding a glass of wine. I think I was addicted to attention, too. I was always dancing on tables and saying really inappropriate things for shock value. This loud girl drunk persona just wasn't me anymore. Newly sober, I acquired a quiet confidence. I knew I was behaving sanely and appropriately. I could never guarantee my behavior once I picked up a drink. I now took pride in the way I conducted myself, and my word was good as gold.

7

At two-plus years sober, I decided to try my hand at online dating. In early recovery, I only dated guys in the program with over ten years of sobriety. I wasn't taking any chances. In my mind, these relationships were always temporary and not what I was looking for long-term. I wasn't in love, so I didn't feel insecure or emotionally vulnerable. It always felt like I had one foot out the door. I was shocked to learn that members with over a decade in recovery were not always happy, joyous, and free. Many were dry, miserable, and condescending. One guy told me that the only reason he didn't drink was that there was no way he would allow me to have more sober time than him. Another told me that he would think of ways to kill himself in his garage and make it look like an accident. It was sad and alarming to learn that members with long-term sobriety were this fucked up. It made me want to work really hard at staying spiritual. I knew that if I lost my connection, I could end up just as wretched as them.

My aunt married a doctor she'd met on eHarmony, so I thought I would give it a whirl. I had no interest in getting married again. I had two drunken failed marriages behind me and wasn't looking for anything serious. I simply thought online dating would cut down on time. How else would I meet someone? I really didn't want to date anyone in the program. I was in love with AA and very selfishly wanted it to be all mine. I didn't want to share the fellowship with a partner. AA is my safe place when the shit hits the fan, and I really didn't want anyone to interfere with my safe haven. I also refused to date anyone from work. A manager told me early on, "Don't shit where you eat." I intuitively knew exactly what this meant, and I wasn't going to let anyone interfere with my livelihood either.

I didn't realize that dating would wake up my ego and allow my false self to run the show again. I created a dating profile, posting flattering pictures and sharing information about myself designed to impress potential suitors. I was basically trying to sell myself, and this stirred up a lot of insecurity. I shared that I never drank alcohol at all, not even on special occasions. I thought this would turn off a lot of guys, especially the ones who still liked to party. Not a chance. I was amazed to find out how many guys want a girl who doesn't drink. It turns out that what I thought was a turnoff was actually a turn-on to many. Also, after years of not giving a shit, I was starting to take pride in my physical appearance. Ready or not, I was joining the land of the living again.

I finally felt whole. God and the AA fellowship had filled a hole inside of me that alcohol never could. My mother, who died depressed and morbidly obese, had asked me a few days before she died, "Do you know why I'm fat?" This question made me so uncomfortable that I was in the process of mumbling something incoherent when she answered her own question. She explained, "I'm fat because I have a hole inside of me, and putting food in it makes it feel better." I was speechless. This emotional bluntness was out of character for my mother, but she wanted me to know this about her. I also think it was her way of relating to my drinking. She was astute enough to realize that I was doing the exact same thing with alcohol. I wish my mother would have found Overeaters Anonymous meetings. I believe that if my mother would have had the privilege of joining OA, there is a very good chance she would still be alive today. I wish spirituality could have healed her too.

I certainly wasn't looking for someone to complete me. I think that "You complete me" line from *Jerry Maguire* is horse shit and a recipe for codependent dysfunction. Due to a lot of internal work, I finally felt complete in my own right. I had love in my heart, I was making great money, and I ran my own household. I didn't feel comfortable dating unless I was making my own money. I was proud to be self-sufficient after living with financial insecurity for years. I know how shitty it feels to be struggling financially, and I wasn't going into a new relationship broke. That's no fun for anyone. I really didn't know what I was looking for. I thought going on some dates would be fun and would help me reach a new level in my sobriety. Because I used to drink over failed romance, however, I was well aware that I was branching out into unchartered waters by dating sober. I knew I had God and AA as my life jacket, though, and I thought I was ready.

8

Sober dating made me very nervous. I was always comfortable meeting someone for drinks—meeting anyone for drinks. No problem. I knew in advance that I would be completely comfortable as long as I was drinking. The eHarmony dating questionnaire asked about frequency of alcohol consumption. The answers varied from daily to a couple times a week, a couple times a month, special occasions, or never. Even though my dates knew in advance that I didn't drink, I still felt inferior. I felt like dating me would be the less-fun option. A friend in the program pointed out that there are more people on the planet who don't drink than who do. I still felt uncomfortable, but I also felt strong in my conviction to stay sober. It's a lot easier to stay sober than to get sober, and there was no way I was giving up on my sobriety. "I don't drink" is a very powerful statement.

I was still living in Indiana, and I dated local guys first. eHarmony allows you to select a dating radius, and I started close to home. I did not specify that I would only date guys who didn't drink. I did not want to only date from the dry-guy short-list; I was keeping my options open. The first guy I liked wanted to meet in a bar attached to a nice restaurant. It was the middle of the afternoon, and we were the only two people in the joint. He ordered a cocktail, and I had a club soda with lime. I'd decided months ago that club soda with lime was going to be my "bar drink," and I was sticking to the plan. My addiction to a legal substance was not going to curtail me socially. I will go anywhere neither cocky nor afraid, I'd resolved.

My date was good-looking, friendly, and successful. Back when I was drinking, talking to guys in bars was like breathing to me. I fancied myself a complete natural, and I believed I was so good that I could teach a class on it. Sober, sipping my club soda, having the "get to know you" conversation felt completely unnatural. I was so grateful I'd remembered to wear a dark-colored top so he couldn't see my pit stains from sweating profusely. I only wanted to disclose things about myself that I wanted him to know. He knew that I didn't drink because I used to have a problem with it. To what extent was none of his business, I decided. He invited me on a pub crawl he was organizing in Chicago. I declined, feeling confused about why a guy in charge of a pub crawl wanted to date a woman who doesn't drink. For crying out loud, experiencing the dating scene sober felt like a special kind of living hell. I couldn't wait for this date to be over. He wanted to see me again, though, and I knew he would call. Even though I was struggling, I put on a good show and he didn't have a clue. I felt like I was stepping back into a war zone of insecurity.

There was no way I was going to make it in the dating world without letting my ego come out and play. I no longer live in my ego, but I see it as an instrument that I can pick up and play like a violin. It's not always such a bad thing. I would suggest allowing your ego to show up on a first date or even a job interview. It's undeniable that a strong ego can advance your career or place in the world. My ego is happy as long as it is engaged. It will tell me that nobody loves me or that I am king of the world. Drunk or sober, my ego can convince me that I am the baddest bitch in the room—any room. I am an egomaniac with an inferiority complex or superiority complex, depending on the time of day. My ego wants me filled with self-pride or self-pity, depending on its mood, and I need to be careful with both of these extremes. I never want to be either boastful with false pride or miserable thinking about poor little me. Sober dating gave me an inferiority complex. I kept forcing myself to go on dates, and I wasn't even enjoying myself. It felt like work.

The song and dance of wanting to make a great first impression felt so disingenuous. I would show up all dolled up and dressed to kill. The entire process is sophomoric and shallow. I wasn't being rigorously honest with my dates. I would tell them that I'd quit drinking because it had got out of hand. I did not disclose that I'd been an acute alcoholic for over a decade and was a current member of Alcoholics Anonymous. I would justify this omission as none of their business. I was only looking for a new friend to fool around with. I wasn't looking for love, commitment, or monogamy. My ego had decided not to take these dates seriously so I wouldn't feel so vulnerable. I was surprised to find that I still had severe underlying insecurity even after working all twelve steps. Dating brought it all to the surface.

I expanded my dating radius to include Chicagoland. I wasn't really hitting it off with anyone from Indiana. The great news was that I'd learned I could be around drinking without feeling tempted. I attribute this to getting sober in a house full of alcohol. I never tried to avoid being around a legal substance. It's not like I had to go out and "score" Chardonnay. Alcohol is everywhere, and my job is to be around it comfortably. The idea of avoiding it is unrealistic and would not be sage council for long-term sobriety. I've never understood the recovering alcoholics who can't be around booze. That has got to feel like booze still controls them. I am only powerless over alcohol if I put it in my system. Even if I'm in the same room as an open bar, it has no power over me. My abstinence from alcohol is simply a byproduct of my spirituality.

I married the first guy I met online from Illinois. His name is Adam, and we agreed to meet in Chicago's Greektown on a Sunday night. I had him meet me at Greek Islands at 5:30 so if the date was a bust, I could still make my 8 p.m. meeting in northwest Indiana. I was becoming more confident with my dating skills. The guys I went out with always lit up when they initially saw me, and they all wanted to go out with me again. I was batting a thousand. My ego was alive and well. I drove to the restaurant with really low expectations, however. These dates just felt like going through the motions. I was forcing myself to go on a lot of dates because I wanted sober practice. I needed practice being out and about socially without drinking. I used to let alcohol do the heavy lifting. After a few rounds, King Alcohol was always running the show, and now I wanted a turn. Like anything else in sobriety, I needed practice. Not only was I becoming comfortable in the dating world; it turns out I wasn't half bad. Most importantly, I was indifferent to being around social drinking—I was safe and protected.

Adam was kind, and I really enjoyed his company. It felt like I'd made a new friend. There were no clues notifying me that this was the guy I was going to fall in love with and marry. He started calling me regularly, and we continued to see each other. I liked him because he was respectful and he wasn't pushy with me. Some of the guys I went out with called me relentlessly, but Adam was much more reserved. We hit it off and genuinely liked each other. Before I knew it, I was seeing him exclusively, and this was really exciting for a former recluse like me. The weirdest part of having a boyfriend was when he asked me if I needed anything. It just floored me. As a low-bottom drunk, no one had ever inquired about my needs. I'd gotten used to the idea that nobody cared. I obviously had residual insecurity from my years as a drunken loner. Starting a new relationship felt like I was pouring Miracle-Gro on my character defects.

9

       I remember laughing at the thought of becoming emotionally attached while playing the dating game. My heart felt full with God and the fellowship, and I thought my days of feeling emotionally vulnerable were over. I felt like I was finally in control of my feelings, and there was no way I was going to allow anyone to interfere with my newfound serenity. Boy, was I wrong. Falling in love made me feel like a thirteen-year-old schoolgirl.

       In the past, I drank because I couldn't handle my emotional reality. I started drinking at an early age in an attempt to cope with emotional discomfort, which stunted my emotional growth. I knew I was different than my fellow human beings by the way I drank and the way I felt. When I first heard the words "emotional disorders" in a meeting, I knew that's what was wrong with me. I knew I felt everything so much more deeply than others, which can be a blessing and a curse. Drinking was just a symptom. I commonly referred to booze as my liquid armor. I felt I needed it because I was emotionally maladjusted and bruised so easily inside.

I came to realize that I wasn't just an alcoholic; I was also an empath. Empaths are extremely sensitive and have aerobic empathy, meaning they take in other people's pain. I have always absorbed other people's pain and emotions and could experience those things right along with them. Many empaths are alcoholics or addicts, choosing to numb themselves to deal with their emotional hypersensitivity. Empaths feel things first, then overthink everything. We are constantly being influenced and affected by other people's energies, emotions, and moods. Because of our overwhelming emotions, we are looking for ways to numb ourselves and cope; therefore many of us distract ourselves with an addiction. Simply put, we are experiencing much more than the average person. This explained the isolation and difficult emotions I experienced, and how other people so easily affected me.

Am I hypersensitive because I'm an alcoholic, or am I an alcoholic because I'm hypersensitive? It's like the chicken and the egg—it sounds like a silly question, but upon reflection, it's not. Many empaths self-medicate with alcohol to block out and protect themselves from emotional overstimulation and hypersensitivity. The immediate relief is undeniable and this "solution" feels effective enough to repeat daily. Our brains engage in the habit of dulling feelings without evaluating the consequences. We use alcohol as a shield from not only our own heartache, emotional turmoil, and nervous systems, but from other people's as well. When intoxicated, the empath feels more of his own emotions and less of everybody else's. Many years of alcohol abuse and violent detoxing certainly did a number on my nervous system. Alcohol is not a viable solution for emotional overload, but a recipe for disaster.

If empathy is really the highest form of intelligence, then I never wanted to be this smart. The trademark of an empath is absorbing and feeling other people's emotions. The ability to feel other people's pain, fear, and suffering is not easy. It requires an absence of ego and inexplicable understanding, and it can be exceedingly taxing on the empath. I have always first felt things intuitively and have had a difficult time comprehending my overwhelming feelings.

There are five different types of empaths: the emotional empath, the medical (physical) empath, the nature empath, the knowing empath, and the spiritual empath. I identify as an emotional empath, the most common type. As an emotional empath, I can easily absorb the emotions of people around me and even experience other people's emotions as my own.

Emotional empaths can be just as loving and supportive as we can be sensitive. The main advantage of being an emotional empath is the level of compassion we can offer others. Compassion is essential for walking in love and establishing true connections. Empaths tend to be incredible listeners with a full range of emotional expression. People always have and always will gravitate to us. Other people are exceptionally drawn to empaths and enjoy being in our presence. It is not unusual for us to isolate, even in sobriety, because of emotional overload.

10

     Falling in love sober felt like falling in love for the first time. I was forty and felt like a giddy teenager. I hadn't been looking for love, and I felt really surprised I'd found someone I wanted to be with. I had a lot of love to give, and it felt good. My business was booming, too. I was professionally successful and had found someone to love. Sobriety looked good on me. Things were going so well that fear crept in, and I began waiting for the other shoe to drop. I wasn't used to success of any kind, so I kept waiting for the seemingly inevitable bad news. I shared my sense of dread with a friend in the program. He told me that I was a new person now and I shouldn't have the same life expectations I'd had as a drunk.

     Adam and I eloped in Destin, Florida. While growing up, my family had a condo in

Destin, and it remains one of my favorite places in the world. Destin offers stunning white beaches with beautiful emerald-green water. We got married on the beach. It was a lovely time—Adam played golf and I sunbathed. I couldn't have asked for anything more.

Paige and I moved in with Adam in Deerfield, Illinois, just one town over from where I grew up. I was sad to say goodbye to my Indiana apartment. I was still working in Indiana, so I continued to hit my high-noon AA meeting, but I was now living over an hour away from my AA peeps. There is something so special about the people we get sober with. They saw changes in me long before I ever saw them in myself. I knew I would find good meetings in Illinois, but there is nothing like attending meetings with the people who watched you get sober. I love AA, and I feel more comfortable in a meeting than anyplace else in the world. The meetings in Indiana still remain my favorite, and probably always will.

Falling in love with my husband was magical, but it also scared the shit out of me.

I felt that falling in love with him meant that he now had the power to hurt me. I felt like I was giving him the power to destroy me, but trusting him not to. Not only was I still struggling with profound insecurity; I was also nervous that if I got my heart broken, I could end up drinking again. My life was getting good and I was scared, because I didn't know what to expect. My life had been a disaster for a long time, and I'd become comfortable in the chaos because I was used to it. In recovery, good, positive changes can feel so scary because living well seems foreign. As horrible as my life was before recovery, it was familiar and pretty predictable. As a drunk, my life went like this: different day, same painful, bullshit behavior. These bad days turned into years and established a pattern. I was on a new path now, establishing a pattern of good days, which requires patience and time. Revolutionary changes don't happen overnight. Time takes time.

Married life in Deerfield was great. My daughter was flourishing in her new school. She made new friends and looked forward to going every morning. Adam and I continued to get along well, and our home life was harmonious. We even adopted a puppy. I was a wife, a mother, and a national producer in business. Everything I'd prayed for was showing up, and I started attending fewer AA meetings. Initially, I didn't like the meetings in Illinois. In Indiana, the chairperson always asked the group for a discussion topic, which meant that anyone could show up at a meeting and have their issue addressed. If I was upset about something, I could show up at a meeting, raise my hand, and the group would discuss my topic. This format was especially helpful in early sobriety. In Illinois, the chairperson gave a "lead" and the group would discuss that subject. *What the hell is this?* I thought. It provided no outlet for the alcoholic who shows up at a meeting with a burning desire to talk about something specific. Additionally, some of these meetings didn't even resemble the old-school Alcoholics Anonymous meetings I was accustomed to. People were allowed to talk about anything they wanted, including drugs, with no admonishment from the chairperson. I had to double-check the directory to ascertain that I was actually in an Alcoholics Anonymous meeting. In Illinois, it felt like AA stood for Addictions Anonymous.

I knew I was attending fewer AA meetings, but I thought I was okay because I had no desire to drink. I thought I was "safe." What I failed to realize is how badly I still needed to go to meetings in order to continue learning how to live sober. I thought fewer meetings was just part of my natural progression. I thought the whole point of going to AA was to *get* a life, not for the program to *become* my life. I'd gone to thousands of meetings in my first couple years. It was like my sobriety was an insurance policy and each meeting was a premium payment. Now, I felt like all of those meetings I'd gone to early on were paying off, and I could relax. I became complacent. I still had the ability to justify any destructive behavior in my head. Attending fewer meetings was a bad idea. Even though I wasn't drinking, my thinking started going downhill fast. I started taking my sobriety for granted.

I have never attended a bad AA meeting. Some are better than others, but I always leave with love and gratitude in my heart. Meetings keep me plugged in to the solution. When I stopped going to my regular meetings, I started experiencing signs of untreated alcoholism. I became restless, irritable, and discontent. I was backpedaling in my recovery. My insecurity went through the roof, and my ego was calling the shots. My relationship with God wasn't as strong as it had been, and this caused all of my other relationships to suffer, especially the one with myself. Alcoholism is a spiritual sickness, and not going to meetings meant I wasn't taking my medicine.

11

Around this time, I found out that my husband was having a relationship with another woman behind my back. Apparently it wasn't a physical affair, but I think finding out about an emotional affair is even worse for someone like me. She sent him a text, and when I grabbed his phone, it was locked. I went to unlock it with his passcode (the date we first met), and he had changed it. Immediately, my heart sank and my stomach began aching. I didn't want to drink. I wanted to jump out of my own skin. I went on to discover that she had come to town and visited him without my knowledge. I always trusted him to travel and see concerts. She was a younger party girl that he'd met at these concerts. I was hurt to the core, and I felt so stupid.

I could not stand the way I felt. I would fluctuate between hurt and anger. It was all I could think about. I was pissed off every morning when I opened my eyes. I lost my zest for life. I could feel the hurt and anger morphing into depression. My feelings of hurt and anger felt infinite; I was drowning in misery. I wanted to know details, and this just made things worse. Whatever one focuses on grows magnified in one's life. The more I learned, the more I thought about it. It was like not being able to change the channel in my mind. If there was one thing that I thought could make me drink, this was it.

He told me that she was just a friend. He told me that he needed a female perspective about our relationship. This didn't help. I knew we'd been going through a rough patch, but the secrecy of all of this happening behind my back felt really bad. I didn't call my sponsor, read my literature, or go to a meeting. I just sat at home by myself, feeling awful. Instead of even trying to make myself feel better, I just sat around engaging in self-inflicted misery. I was mad, and I thought a lot about getting even. I wanted both of them to suffer. I was purposely abusing myself again, but this time with thoughts. These strong feelings of anger and inability to forgive were killing me, and I kept feeding them all fucking day. The self-abuse merry-go-round was operational again and back in business.

I was isolating, and I was miserable. I was having the same pity parties I'd had as a drunk, but this time without booze. I was officially an unhappy dry alcoholic. I had reached a new and different kind of bottom. I didn't want to drink and I didn't want to die, but I was seriously depressed. My heart felt like a battered punching bag, abandoned on the side of the road, and my mind was fuming with anger and plotting revenge. My ego was thrilled that I was absorbed in self-pity and built a wall separating me from God. The funny thing about my depression is that I was in no hurry to snap out of it. I knew I was in dangerous territory and didn't make a move. I knew depression had killed my mother, and I was still too depressed to even want to get better. I was sleeping a lot and had zero motivation.

Intellectually, I knew what to do to make myself feel better, and I forced myself to get to work. For the record, I didn't feel like doing any of the work to try to get out of this funk. I didn't have the energy, emotionally or physically. I just didn't feel like it. If I would've waited until I felt like doing something about my depression, I would still be in bed, crying in my pajamas. But depression can't hit a moving target, I knew. I used to run and work out, though that seemed overly ambitious in my current condition. Instead, I started small and reluctantly. I forced myself to start walking around the block every morning. I hated every second of it—even tying my running shoes felt like a chore. But I forced myself to continue daily, regardless of how I felt.

My morning walk began getting easier and becoming a habit. Habits create new disciplines. After my walk, I started hitting a morning meeting. I went to a new meeting where I didn't know anyone. I'd forgotten all about the comfort and the feeling of belonging that only AA meetings can offer. It was great to be around people, and it gave me a chance to get out of myself. It provided a much-needed break from my self-inflicted misery and self-centered fear. My depression had made me exceedingly selfish. I felt shitty, so it was hard to see past my pain. I would be the last one to show up at the meeting and the first one to leave. I was an AA thief. I listened to all the wisdom in the room and ran out of there as fast as I could. I felt like shit and didn't want to talk to anyone, but I kept coming back.

12

Drinking or not, left to my own devices I am self-destructive. After years in recovery, I learned that my drinking problem was really just a thinking problem all along. I was depressed because I was hurt and angry. I was pissed and felt entitled to my rage. I was justifying my anger instead of taking responsibility for it. Most angry people feel their anger is justified; therefore, they won't take responsibility for dealing with it. Righteous indignation is a reactive emotion of feeling wronged. Since I used to be a slave to the behavioral patterns of acute alcoholism, I was overly familiar with playing the victim and sitting around feeling sorry for myself. I did it for years.

After attending thousands of AA meetings, I know that acceptance is the answer to all of my problems. In order to be happy, I need to practice acceptance. I don't have to like something or approve of it, but I need to accept it in order to move on. I was still in disbelief about what had happened in my relationship, and this kept me in denial. I didn't want to believe things that would hurt my feelings. I kept asking questions, hoping that the answers would be different and I could chalk this up as one big misunderstanding. My thirst for different answers was desperate and pathetic, and it kept me stuck. I knew I needed to accept my situation as it was; anything else would be avoidance of reality. Acceptance was mandatory for me to move forward, yet I couldn't embrace my reality. Why was I doing this to myself? What was I holding on to? Was I hurting myself on purpose?

I needed to practice acceptance and forgiveness, but I really didn't want to. In my anger, forgiveness wasn't even on my radar. Forgiveness is very hard for me; it doesn't even feel like it's part of my constitutional makeup. I was holding on tight to my resentment and didn't want to let go. I couldn't let go of my resentment because I was using it as a defense mechanism. My ego thought that as long as I stayed pissed and didn't accept the offense as reality, I could avoid the hurt. My ego was trying to protect me by holding on to anger. Feeling angry can feel more powerful than feeling sad and vulnerable. My ego flourishes in the pain and relishes in the self-pity. Holding on to the resentment was fueling my ego, and I had no idea. I just stayed pissed and stuck.

Though I knew this anger was killing me, I didn't know how to shake it. Harboring resentment made me powerless over the situation and my own feelings. I wanted to live a life that wasn't dominated by unresolved anger, hate, and resentment. I wanted to take my power back, but I was up against a thousand forms of fear. Falling in love had made me feel vulnerable and insecure. Nothing awakens distant hurts like a close relationship. Intellectually, I know that I am solely responsible for my happiness. Blaming Adam for my unhappiness let me play the victim and avoid personal responsibility. Alcoholics are known to have an appalling lack of perspective. My focus is always on what happened to me. I rarely like to look at my part in a difficult situation. I didn't yet consider that maybe my problem wasn't who had wronged me, but what I was doing wrong.

13

I wasn't going to get any better as long as I kept playing the victim. I was not entirely innocent in the situation; I just refused to look at my part. I was the one who responded with hurt, anger, and blame, which made me stressed out and depressed. I was scared that if I let go of the resentment, I would wind up drowning in heartache and helplessness. I wanted to be in charge of my own emotional world. I wanted to take my power back and make healthy choices with my feelings and behaviors. However, I had no emotional control, and it was easier to blame someone else for my inability to cope. Blaming someone else for my rage was a complete cop-out and wiped out any chance for personal improvement. I had to give up blame if I ever wanted to be happy.

In active alcoholism, I'd lost the power of choice in drink. My body demanded it, and I continued to feed the beast. I had no willpower, and I even convinced myself that I needed to keep drinking in order to continue living. As an angry, dry drunk, I once again lost the power of choice—this time, over my emotions. Healing comes from taking responsibility. I needed to take an honest look at myself and decide if I wanted to continue blaming others and feeling sorry for myself. Blaming others is counterproductive, because it actually makes us feel worse. I had to admit that I'd given my power away and I am the only one who is 100% responsible for my feelings and actions.

I needed to change my thinking if I didn't want to keep cycling through the same negative experiences. I chose to see the situation as an opportunity for personal growth instead of a painful problem with no solution. Dwelling on the problem had magnified it and caused more stress. Seeing the problem as an opportunity to learn and grow changed my focus. Looking at the problem as an opportunity felt less intimidating and contextualized the situation.

This mental shift helped me gain objectivity. I was able to see the problem as a separate entity, which diminished its power over me. Skillful observation allowed me to see my unwanted thoughts and emotions without letting them take over. This new focus gave me the ability to adopt a problem-solving mindset.

I knew I needed to learn how to forgive in order to really enjoy my life, and here was my chance. Again, forgiveness historically has not been one of my strong suits. When wronged, I would just walk away. I just cut the person who offended me out of my life, and the grudge would soften over time. I was sick and tired of carrying around resentment, though, because it was destroying my mental health. Selfishly, I wanted to learn to forgive solely for me. I was sick and tired of self-inflicted misery. The sad reality was that I was still hurting myself—not with booze, but with destructive thinking. I was stuck in mental slavery and believed forgiveness was my key to freedom.

Forgiveness sounded great in theory, but the idea of practicing it felt impossible.

When someone wrongs me, revenge feels like the solution and forgiveness feels like asking the impossible. I want to get mad and I want to get even. Now, I just wanted to get better, and forgiveness was the clear solution. By forgiving, I learned, I am accepting the reality of what happened and not attaching anger to the situation. I am exercising self-control with my emotions. This is a constant exercise in thought control. I decided to retrain my brain not to feel upset when an offense comes into my mind. This is an effective practice because forgiveness is not an event. It is a constant new attitude that becomes familiar with a lot of practice.

14

Some people like to call AA a cult that brainwashes people. This doesn't bother me. If AA is brainwashing, then I'm grateful for the scrubbing. Alcoholics Anonymous first changed my thinking, then changed my life. Resentment was just another thinking problem that I needed to change. I did not want to focus on my resentment anymore. Every time resentment popped into my head, I quickly dismissed it and refused to engage. I was done overthinking about and focusing on it. I'd been using it as a distraction so I wouldn't have to take responsibility for myself and my own happiness. To counteract my mental obsession with alcohol, I'd dismissed the thought of a drink every single time it crossed my mind. I would not engage in and romanticize thoughts about alcohol. I believe that God removed my mental obsession, but not without my cooperation. Now, I asked for

God's help with my resentment too, and I cooperated by immediately dismissing resentful thoughts as soon as they popped up.

I've experienced a psychic change in the way that I see alcohol. I used to see it as my best friend and my lifesaver. I now see it as a dangerous foe that wants me dead. I have also experienced a psychic change in the way I see resentment. I used to welcome the thought of resentment and wallow in self-pity. Now, I see the thought of resentment as a clear and present danger to my happiness and serenity. Overthinking causes unhappiness, and I just couldn't take the misery anymore. I was committed to doing the work to avoid being a prisoner of miserable thinking. Everybody knows what it's like to be pestered with unwanted thoughts. The key is to have a strategy in advance. I stopped attaching anger to my resentment, and I would immediately replace a negative thought with a positive one. Instead of thinking about something painful from the past, I would switch my focus to my growth and happiness. I took my power back by admitting that there is nothing to gain from hurtful reflection and by making a commitment to my personal growth and happiness by no longer engaging in the negativity. The negative thoughts became less and less frequent, and the art of turning negative thinking into positive thinking became easier, with practice and a firm commitment.

I can't do anything successfully without God. Forgiveness is not in my DNA. That's why I asked God to help me with forgiveness, and this required even more cooperation on my part. I prayed for months about it, asking God to change me into a more forgiving person. At first, I did not change; I just continued feeling angry every day. Then God asked me to change for Him. I know that I am nothing without God. I honor my relationship with my Higher Power beyond description, and this was something I could do for God. I needed to show my obedience to God by forgiving. I still believe forgiveness is impossible for me to do on my own, but all things are possible with God. Alcoholics are exceedingly selfish, but I know God wants me to live my life with an open heart by loving and forgiving other people. By not forgiving other people, I wasn't living in obedience to God. My disobedience was of my own doing and ensured a life of anger and misery. It astounds me that I didn't catch this sooner. I'd begged for God to help me with my drinking problem. Not only did He help me quit drinking; He also filled my heart with love and showed me a beautiful way to live. The whole idea of walking in love is to have love flowing in and out of me all day. Learning forgiveness is an integral part of a successful spiritual life in which one experiences this love. I needed to learn how to forgive in order to continue trudging the road to a happy destiny. I learned to forgive because I love God. God forgives me and wants me to forgive others. By continually practicing forgiveness, I am honoring God and enjoying my life.

I felt so unlovable for so long. I even felt worthless and unlovable to God. This all resurfaced when I fell in love in sobriety. Falling in love released insecurities I wasn't even aware I had. I think my resentment of my husband was a very complicated and layered situation. He ended his relationship with his female friend, and I eventually forgave him. My emotional disorder convinced me that he loved her more than he'd ever loved me, because I was unlovable. When overly emotional, my thinking is wacky and blows everything out of proportion. My husband's transgression shone a light on my emotional immaturity. Alcoholism had stunted my emotional growth, as those of us who abuse alcohol from an early age typically experience problems with emotional maturity. Falling in love sober was scary and wonderful, but I was unprepared. I'd had relationships while I was drinking, but I wasn't really a participant in them. The sad truth is that as a drunk, I wasn't even a participant in my own life, which made it impossible to participate in a relationship.

Feeling inexperienced in a relationship was another blow to my already compromised self-esteem. After getting sober and working all twelve steps, my ego diminished and my self-esteem was healthy. I was plugged into the program and feeling good about myself. Attending fewer meetings and having a new marriage had released my ego and triggered my profound insecurity. I was depending less on God and more on myself. I started shouldering the burdens of feeling responsible for a happy life and successful marriage. I prioritized my marriage and started to lose myself in codependency. I was still looking outside of myself for validation, this time from my relationship. I could sense my partner's wants and needs and would put them before my own. I would focus on situations from my partner's perspective instead of my own. Like many emotional empaths, I was experiencing symptoms of codependency.

My ego and insecurity were back in full force. I knew I still carried around a lot of insecurity from all those years as a low-bottom drunk. God and the fellowship had loved me back to life, and if I'm not living in the solution, fear and self-loathing come back into play. Many women in recovery still struggle with their sense of self-worth. When I went to a women's AA retreat in Akron, Ohio, I was shocked to meet many beautiful women in recovery who were still afflicted with low self-esteem. Low self-esteem is the leading cause of alcohol addiction, and as the addiction gets worse, the self-esteem gets lower and lower. Low self-esteem is consistent among both male and female alcoholics, but it's especially prevalent among acute female alcoholics.

There is a huge discrepancy between my ego and my self-worth. I thought I had healthy self-esteem before I fell in love. It was disconcerting to discover that underneath my protective ego, I am an immature and inexperienced little girl who is desperate to be loved. I was so insecure that I had trouble believing that my husband really loved me. My ego could convince me that I am the greatest thing since sliced bread and that he's really the lucky one, but underneath all the bullshit, I felt unworthy of a loving relationship. I was self-sabotaging my recovery without alcohol, because someplace deep down, I felt that I didn't deserve to be happy.

15

It was time to get back to basics. I'd tried running my life again and was screwing it up. I needed to put God back in charge. My life works best when God is in the driver's seat and I'm just another bozo on the bus enjoying the ride. First, I needed to wholeheartedly believe that God loves me. Without God's unconditional love as my foundation, I struggle with caring for myself and the wheels fall off. I must fundamentally believe that God loves me in order to practice any type of self-love or self-care. It is imperative for me to believe that God loves me and that I am worth loving. I must put my trust in God, not in my emotions, as they can deceive me and steer me off course. My fear of abandonment caused me to look outside of myself for love and comfort, but with God, my strength and confidence grow internally. God gives me the ability to love myself and find comfort and safety inside. My fear of abandonment will lie to me, saying I need to find love and acceptance elsewhere. Thus, I must constantly reaffirm that God loves me unconditionally and will never leave me.

Pain sucks, but pain is where the growth is. Wisdom is nothing more than healed pain. I'd hit my emotional bottom, and I was done digging. I was determined to reclaim my happiness and walk in love. I am no longer interested in looking back on events that have caused me pain. Negative thinking is a form of self-sabotage that delivers disastrous results. Like alcoholism, negative thoughts are a huge obstacle to overcome. I now realize how powerful my thoughts are. Sometimes it's not even the hurt that makes us suffer, but all the negativity we attach to the pain. Emotional health starts with awareness of my thoughts, feelings, and behaviors. Exerting control over my emotions instead of allowing them to control me has helped me cope with stress and trouble in a positive way. Learning how to control your fear is learning how to live free from it.

Learning the power of forgiveness has changed my life. Not only am I able to forgive others; I also forgive myself. If God believes that I am lovable and worthy of forgiveness, then I should, too. Forgiving myself is not about forgetting; it's about letting go of past mistakes. The past is over. It cannot be erased or edited, only accepted. Increased acceptance generates emotional healing. My self-esteem was suffering because I hadn't completely forgiven myself for my past choices. Radical acceptance of myself and my past mistakes catalyzed my movement into something greater. I had to stop buying into the enemy's bullshit. There are negative forces at work, and beautiful things happen when we distance ourselves from them. I wanted to live my best life possible, and not forgiving one's self leads to self-destruction. I forgive myself for wasting so many years inebriated, and I forgive myself for not knowing what I didn't know until I learned it. Forgiveness of self and others was integral in rebuilding my self-esteem. Forgiveness softens my emotions and gives me a choice. I ask myself, "Do I want to feel disturbed by focusing on my past?" Exercising control over focusing on past hurts empowers me and eradicates my victim mentality. I therefore found my personal strength in forgiveness.

I was not thrilled to discover I was an empath, but it made sense. As early as childhood, I remember being able to take on other people's emotions as if they were my own. I assumed this was normal and that everybody else had this ability too. It turns out that roughly one in twenty people has this ability (or affliction), because we were born this way. We are highly attuned to other people's moods and energies, which can be overwhelmingly stressful and even dangerous. We feel everything to the extreme and can suffer from emotional overwhelm. We internalize stressful emotions and overthink our feelings. My destructive drinking was just a poor coping mechanism gone awry for handling my larger-than-life feelings. Being this sensitive made me feel different and less understood, so I would search for comfort in alcohol, which made it all worse.

I am always going to be an alcoholic. I can change a lot of things about myself, but I can't change the way I drink alcohol. There is no cure for alcoholism, but I can arrest the drinking and treat my symptoms with spirituality and self-love. I really hope I never drink again, but after years of treatment, I can guarantee I would not enjoy it. A head full of AA and a belly full of booze is no place I want to be. I believe the program of Alcoholics Anonymous has effectively screwed up my drinking.

Like being an alcoholic, I am always going to be an empath. Empaths are born, not made. I did not grow up in a society that valued sensitivity, so instead of exploring my feelings, I tried to drown them out. My innate ability to feel the emotions of others has been with me as long as I can remember. Instead of numbing these feelings with an addiction, I needed to take a sober look at my emotional state and figure out what's been going on.

16

My mother and I had an exceptionally close relationship. She wasn't just my mother. She was my best friend, my life coach, and my cheerleader. Even as a little girl, I can remember picking up on her sadness as my own. My mother's obesity caused her to carry around a lot of shame. Naturally, I carried her shame too as my own. I never even suspected this was abnormal. It started to dawn on me that maybe one of the reasons I was so emotionally maladjusted is that I was carrying around other people's emotions as well as my own. Picking up on other people's emotions, thoughts, and experiences is not only confusing, but also quite damaging. Unknowingly absorbing the stress and pain of others causes many empaths to suffer severely. This emotional contagion can cause anxiety, depression, debilitating confusion, and self-doubt.

Because I was unaware of my ability, I did not see a need to protect myself.

Most empaths exhibit signs of codependency. Codependency is a learned behavior and coping mechanism that results in a dysfunctional relationship. The term "codependent" used to imply enabling an addicted person, but modern-day understanding refers to extreme dependence on a specific relationship. Codependence is usually based on low self-esteem. Core symptoms of codependency include lack of self-worth, difficulty with self-care, and trouble setting personal boundaries. Most empaths struggle with codependency, but not all codependents are empaths. I experienced codependency first in my relationship with my late mother, and later in my marriage after I quit drinking. In both of these relationships, I had an excessive emotional and psychological reliance on someone else.

Like alcoholism, codependency gives me a distraction so I can avoid looking at myself and taking responsibility for my life. When I am more focused on my partner's wants or needs than my own, that prevents me from taking an honest look at myself and my circumstances. In active addiction, I went to great lengths to avoid self-reflection and taking responsibility. Historically, avoidance has always been one of my coping mechanisms. Giving another person excessive emotional or psychological attention distracts me from my own self-improvement. I become too busy worrying about what that person needs and feels to think about what *I* need to do. If I'm getting my self-esteem and emotional needs met by my partner, then I can be lazy and not practice self-love. Constantly practicing self-love can be challenging, and reverting back to old destructive ways is easy. To get out of this pattern, I need to focus on my own journey and my soul's purpose. Without self-examination, it's easy to fall back into old traps.

Codependency definitely fueled my anger, too. By focusing my time and energy on my husband's mistakes, I gave myself less time to look at my own. I'd made plenty of mistakes that I still felt bad about, and I would much rather focus on my husband's faults than taking an honest look at my own.

Focusing on my husband's mistakes prolonged my anger and kept me stuck. I now know there is no hope for self-improvement if I'm still pointing the finger at someone else and ducking responsibility. I am fully responsible for my own happiness, and blaming someone else is a waste of time. I learned the hard way that playing the victim kept me stuck in dysfunction.

17

       Empaths are no strangers to dysfunction. Many empaths find themselves in dysfunctional relationships involving codependency, abuse, or parasitic partners. Once a realized I was an empath, I started seeking out other empaths to exchange notes. I intuitively knew who to talk to (a little empath humor, but it's true). I have picked up a lot from sitting in countless AA meetings throughout the years. I am never passive in a meeting. I am not there to pass time and play on my phone. I am actively watching and listening to every member. This active participation has turned me into an amateur cultural anthropologist. I've gotten so good at studying other people's behaviors, I feel like a human lie detector test. Some of my empath friends have also experienced codependency in their relationships, but I was blown away by the number of empaths who have experienced a relationship with a narcissist. The overwhelming number of empaths in recovery who have been in a relationship with a narcissist blew me away.

Narcissists seek out empaths as targets because of the empaths' giving nature. They are attracted to the people they will get the biggest use from. Narcissistic personality disorder (NPD) is a condition in which a person has an inflated sense of self-importance. I used to think that a narcissist was just someone with a big ego, but narcissism is so much more than that. People with NPD have grandiose delusions, lack authentic empathy, have an overwhelming need for admiration, and are self-centered, arrogant, manipulative, and demanding. Empaths and narcissists are often drawn to each other. Empaths are natural caregivers, and narcissists will take full advantage. Narcissists feel no guilt about manipulating empaths in exchange for control. The more love and understanding the empath offers, the more powerful the narcissist becomes. For that reason, many refer to narcissists as emotional vampires. They are selfish emotional manipulators who aim to get what they want to serve their own agenda. They are excellent actors, faking respect, concern, and even love. They use other people to try to fill a void inside that they can never fill themselves. They are people addicts who feed off of others because they have nothing coming from within to nourish them.

The relationship between the empath and the narcissist is doomed. The narcissist is highly skilled at making a great first impression, typically coming off as charming, caring, and personable. This is all a well-crafted facade that they cannot maintain in the long-term. It simply gets the empath "hooked." The empath tends to believe that other people are also honest and sincere, and the narcissist preys on this belief. During this early phase, the narcissist typically "love bombs" the empath. Love bombing is an attempt to disarm the empath's natural defenses by showering the empath with love, affection, and adoration. The narcissist comes in hard and fast with lavish declarations of love and affection, hoping to secure the empath's devotion. The empath falls hard, feeling she has found her soulmate and can't believe her good fortune. After the narcissist secures a relationship with an empath, the facade starts to crack and the bogus mask starts to slip. All narcissists have a false persona to cover up weakness and a vulnerability that would be pathetic if it weren't so shockingly cruel.

The relationship cycle of narcissistic abuse includes three stages: idealization, devaluing, and discarding. This cycle can repeat over and over. The idealization or "love bombing" stage can produce emotional highs comparable to a potent drug to secure the empath hook, line, and sinker. The narcissist is highly skilled at making the empath feel loved and special in the beginning. When the narcissist becomes more comfortable, the empath will start to notice signs of devaluation. Many empaths are wearing rose-colored glasses, though, as they are so in love that they have difficulty seeing any red flags. A common tactic during the devaluation stage is gaslighting, a type of abuse in which the narcissist will purposefully confuse the empath to create self-doubt. Gaslighting is one of the most harmful types of emotional and mental abuse. Its purpose is to confuse and disorient the victim, giving the narcissist more control. Gaslighting minimizes and devalues the victim's perception of reality, making the victim feel crazy and easier to manipulate. During devaluation, trauma bonding occurs as the result of ongoing cycles of abuse in which intermittent reinforcement of reward and punishment creates powerful emotional bonds that are resistant to change. This explains why some people stay in abusive situations. Often the victim doesn't even realize she is in one. When the empath is no longer useful to the narcissist, the empath will be discarded like old news. This is usually because the narcissist already has a new supply lined up to take the empath's place. If the narcissist decides that the new supply is superior, the discard could be final. The discard stage is the last part of the cycle, but sometimes the narcissist doesn't discard permanently. It all depends on how valuable the supply (attention) is to the narcissist.

These parasitic relationships can destroy empaths, leaving them emotionally bankrupt. For many, the love they felt during the beginning stages of the relationship felt like the real thing, and finding out it was all bullshit can be devastating. The empath needs to heal the wounds that the narcissist tapped into to begin with. Sometimes these wounds go all the way back to childhood. The narcissist is unable to heal and grow up because narcissists don't face their wounds and evolve. They just find more supply and continue the destruction. Trying to hold the narcissist accountable keeps the empath captivated. The empath needs to take responsibility for the situation, maybe even admitting that she knew on some level that the relationship was a lie. The empath will question her own judgment and feel foolish or even powerless. Blaming or wanting to get even with a narcissist is a waste of time. Healing old wounds, practicing self-love, and setting boundaries are necessities in overcoming narcissistic abuse.

As an active alcoholic, I exhibited narcissistic characteristics. Alcoholics and narcissists share similarities, even though alcoholism is an addiction and narcissism is a personality disorder. Both the active alcoholic and the narcissist are in denial, refusing to look at the destruction they've caused and take responsibility. As a drunk, I lived in survival mode, always focused on my next drink. I was in denial, thinking I was only hurting myself, though I was also scared to acknowledge my self-destruction. Similarly, narcissists are focused on the next attention fix. They will manipulate others to keep feeding their need for attention and praise. Both the narcissist and the active alcoholic are self-absorbed and committed to having their primary needs met, with little to no consideration of others. In both cases, their view of the world is narrow and they can't seem to see beyond their self-centered ways.

18

Apparently, I was born both an alcoholic and an empath. I was not happy or grateful to learn about either one of these conditions. I have learned to treat and manage my alcoholism, but I've never been thrilled about being afflicted in the first place. I hear other grateful alcoholics state that their worst day sober still beats their best day drunk. I had some great times drinking, and I don't share the same sentiment. I came to AA hoping the members could teach me how to drink successfully, but instead I admitted to my innermost self that I am an alcoholic and abstinence is my only option for a successful life. I believe only alcoholics wonder if they're an alcoholic. Social drinkers don't struggle with the same dilemma. If you think you're an alcoholic, there's a very good chance you are. The same goes for being an empath. If you are questioning if you're really an empath, the answer is generally yes. The biggest obstacle for empaths is learning to trust in ourselves and our feelings. There is an odd misconception that someone else must know more than you do, and this self-doubt can get in the way. For empaths, our feelings are our truth. Empaths don't need outside validation and should not rely on other people to co-sign their belief systems.

Many empaths are born self-aware. This is not my story. I figured it out due to the overwhelming and uncontrollable feelings I experienced in sobriety. My emotions felt infinite and ocean-deep. Comprehending that I am an empath was not easy, but it made sense. I believe that my constant need for alone time and the way I distracted myself with an addiction are closely connected to my hypersensitivity. My hypersensitivity has never felt like a gift. My excessive emotions have caused me so many hours of mental anguish, leaving me feeling defective and trapped. These deep feelings were something I wanted to get rid of, not something I felt blessed to experience. I was shocked to learn that other empaths view these feelings as a gift. I just wanted to learn how to deal with them without drinking myself to death or feeling crazed.

As an empath, commingling other people's emotions with my own has been exhausting, draining, and confusing. Learning where someone else ends and I begin seems like a strange exercise, but personal boundaries are imperative for empaths. For some empaths, being surrounded by a lot of people can trigger the absorption of strong emotions such as anger, jealousy, and fear. In extreme cases, these absorbed emotions can be debilitating to the empath, even making him physically sick. I already experience my own emotions to the extreme, and I needed to learn how to separate my own emotions from other people's feelings (which can literally feel like my own). Until recently, I did not realize why I felt I was drowning in an emotional sea and other people did not experience the same intensity of feelings. A fellow empath suggested I focus on meditation to build awareness and shield myself from unwanted energy.

I'm no stranger to meditation. It's an important part of the AA program that my sponsor strongly encouraged when I quit drinking and started working steps. These are just a few life-changing benefits of meditation: It will help you to manage stress, connect to your purpose, lower your blood pressure, attain laser focus, heighten intuition, improve memory, increase your immunity, decrease inflammation, boost your happiness, expand your awareness, decrease anxiety and depression, and cultivate compassion. For the empath, learning to control the mind is essential for a happy life. Our thoughts are directly connected to our feelings. Meditation allows us greater control of what we focus on, and what we focus on grows magnified in our lives. Being an empath struggling with codependency, I needed and wanted to put the focus back on myself. As with everything else that's good for me, I'd stopped meditating when I became angry and depressed. I needed to take action. I started taking private meditation lessons to get back to basics.

My instructor started me on the Subtraction Method. This method is designed to eliminate all the bullshit thinking I'd attached to the events of my life. She had me repeat the mantra, "Please, truth, eliminate the false," while revisiting my entire life, going back to my earliest memories. This exercise made me realize that a lot of thoughts and feelings I'd attached to previous events were just things created by my False Self. The False Self is a defense facade that is developed early on. It's an artificial persona that people create to protect themselves from re-experiencing developmental trauma, shock, and stress in close relationships. This method is groundbreaking and is receiving worldwide buzz because it can completely eliminate the mind of the False Self and allow one to be born as the True Self. When one is reborn in Truth, he experiences the most happiness a human being can have.

In my search for Truth, meditation identified a lot of my unresolved issues. I was an empath who definitely needed firm boundaries. It became apparent that a lot of the painful emotional baggage I was lugging around didn't even belong to me. I learned the importance of not examining other people's thoughts and not taking anything personally. Subtraction meditation alerted me that I was still holding on to my deceased mother's sadness as my own. Awareness brought on by meditation allowed me to set new, life-changing boundaries. I am unwilling to absorb anyone else's energy. I am still very aware of it, but I am unwilling to absorb it. I refuse. If I am unknowingly carrying around someone else's crap, meditation allows me to name it, claim it, and dump it. I've also put the focus back on my joy and my happiness. I relearned and became comfortable with the word "no." In fact, I think the word "no" is a full sentence. I no longer suffer from the disease of needing to please others. I have learned the hard way the importance of putting myself first. My priority is to keep my eyes on my own paper and worry less about what other people are up to.

Meditation has also alerted me that I was carrying around painful unresolved feelings. These feelings weren't attached to any specific memories, just unresolved issues that I needed to address. I was getting really upset about things happening in my current life because they stirred up unhealed feelings from my past. Not only did I need to make peace with my past; I had to rid myself of old, harmful thinking and feeling patterns that were still getting in my way. I needed to come to terms with the fact that I'd lived like a hopeless drunk for over a decade and people treated me accordingly. The fact that I don't blame anyone for treating me like a drunk—because that's precisely what I was—doesn't mean it didn't take a toll on me. My body was shutting down from alcoholism when I surrendered and starting working steps. I knew just enough to put the drink down and learn to walk in love, but not enough to continually stay plugged in to the solution. I'm a real alcoholic, and for me to drink is to die. I had no problem staying abstinent once I became sober, but I had trouble staying happy. My willingness to change was not really a choice, but a reaction to pain.

19

It turns out I'm really good at self-sabotage, even without alcohol. I knew how to get drunk and screw things up. That was a no-brainer, and I did it for years. Many alcoholics drink at the most inopportune times and blow it. These drunken fiascos are so common that they're featured in the AA literature. I had to take an honest look at my self-destruction in sobriety, too. For alcoholics, personal self-sabotage is in our nature. Many of us have given up homes, families, careers, and even our self-respect in exchange for drunken destruction. Non-alcoholics can't even fathom why we burn everything to the ground. Addiction is the epitome of self-sabotage, and addictive people can self-destruct in both addiction and recovery. Self-defeating behaviors become glaring in active addiction and don't magically disappear when we sober up. I wish my character defects had magically vanished like my mental obsession, but removing and managing shortcomings takes constant work and an unshakable trust in God.

Relapse is the most obvious self-sabotaging behavior in recovery, but there are many other self-defeating symptoms that don't involve picking up a drink. We allow old thinking patterns and behaviors to resurface because they are familiar and comfortable. We derail our new healthy lifestyle with fear and self-doubt. We became so accustomed to punishing ourselves in active addiction that we normalized this behavior. Sometimes deep down, we don't believe we deserve to be happy, so we fuck it up. This is the ultimate defiance of healthy, correct thinking. Fear throws us off center and out of wack. It is the energy force behind all of our destructive thoughts and behaviors. When we are avoiding happiness and not appreciating success, we are really avoiding God. God loves us and wants us to be happy, even more than we want it for ourselves. The problem is with us. We struggle to believe that we are worthy of the beautiful life God wants for us, so we miss out by not stepping into it.

I become what I think, and I will never go beyond what I believe. If I don't love myself and believe I am worthy of an amazing life, I am never going to have one. So many of us are waiting on God, but in actuality we have that backward. God is waiting on *us* to fully believe in His love for us in order to step into our destiny. Belief is the most important metric when it comes to living our best lives and being our best selves. We need to believe in God's love for us with every fiber of our being. Not fully understanding and believing how much God loves us is our biggest mistake. If we fully grasped and comprehended His love for us, we would not walk around insecure, self-doubting, worrying, uncomfortable, and scared. We were not created to live defeated, and recycling these negative feelings is not only a waste of energy, but one of the worst habits possible. These negative feelings are a result of not knowing how loved we are by God and that we live in a supportive universe. We will never know the beautiful life God has in store for us if we don't believe.

When you know deep down in your being that God loves you, life becomes really enjoyable. When you finally realize that God has an amazing life planned for you, you can start to relax and enjoy it. When you know the abundance of God's love, it becomes easy to trust in God's will for you and your life. The biggest mistake I have made in recovery was forgetting how much God loves me. When I forget how much God loves me, I start to question the events in my life and stop trusting God completely. This lack of belief and trust is the root of all of my personal problems. Just as I needed to surrender to God for sobriety, I need to surrender to the will of God for happiness. After years of unsuccessfully trying to control my life, I finally learned how to stop, trust, and let go. Let's be frank: We talk a lot of rhetoric about letting go and letting God, but it is amply clear that a lot of us are still carrying around crap that we should've let go of already. There are some things we know we should let go of, but we still torture ourselves with our circumstances because we are scared to relinquish control. This fear of giving up control is the reason why we are miserable.

We are not fooling God, either. God knows what is in our hearts and how much we trust Him.

Trusting God is a lifelong process. When we surrender control and trust in God's plan, beautiful, amazing things start to happen. If we continue trying to take control, we invariably end up frustrated and disappointed. We need to trust that God knows what He is doing and doesn't need any instructions from us. We need to trust God with things we don't understand and believe that God can work out any situation for our highest good. God wants us to trust Him first and foremost in our lives. We need to get in agreement with God if we want Him to work in our lives. Give God permission to bless you with your cooperation and obedience.

The best way to show obedience to God is loving and forgiving other people. It's not always easy, but that's why it's called obedience. I look at it this way: The whole point of my spiritual journey is to allow love to flow in and out of me. Being loving to other people is what makes me useful to God. If I am angry or depressed, I am not serving God, and ultimately this lack of service causes misery. I need to keep my love and trust in God so strong that it wipes out my self-defeating feelings that ruin the quality of my life.

Alcoholics are childish, sensitive, and grandiose. These characteristics cause alcoholics to have personal problems even after working all twelve steps. Many of us put in the work initially to stop drinking and get out of harm's way, but we don't continue the necessary upkeep to live happy, joyous, and free. Most of us come into AA as very sick people. We are maladjusted to life, unhappy, mentally defective, and out of touch with reality. We are so desperate to change in the beginning that we will do anything, but when we start getting better, some of us start slacking off. When we stop working on our recovery, our character defects become more pronounced. In typical alcoholic fashion, we tend to address our problems when the pain becomes too much to handle. People (especially alcoholics) generally don't change until they become really uncomfortable. It is this discomfort that drives the individual to look at personal flaws head-on. Alcoholics struggle with selfishness, dishonesty, self-seeking behavior, and fear. These flaws obstruct our recovery. I alone cannot remove these defects; only God can, but I can't expect God to remove my character flaws if I keep practicing them. We must be entirely ready for God to remove our defects and resist engaging in old thinking patterns and behaviors. We must humble ourselves through prayer and meditation. We must ask for God's help, and our cooperation is necessary for true change to occur. We must stop engaging in our old ways to make room for truly authentic results.

Some of us are sicker than others. AA literature explains that many alcoholics suffer from grave emotional and mental disorders. This is not surprising, considering our liquor was but a symptom and our basic problem is with our thinking. Bill Wilson (cofounder of Alcoholics Anonymous) struggled with depression for decades after he gave up booze, even though he'd created the most powerful self-help movement ever. Despite his wild success, he never claimed to be perfect. He still struggled with dependence on people and situations for security, and when things didn't work out to his specifications, depression set in. I love Bill W. and believe his movement saved my life. He was always looking for solutions for his personal problems and would honestly and openly share his findings with anyone and everyone who was interested. AA encourages getting outside help for those who need it.

I have realized that consistency is the difference between failure and success. Real change in personal improvement requires consistency. I need to keep a constant forgiving attitude toward myself and others to be happy, healthy, and useful. I remain consistent with my morning exercise, as physical exercise is one of the most effective ways to improve mental health. Regular exercise relieves tension, improves mood, and reduces anxiety. Remaining committed to physical exercise is a necessity for my self-esteem. I need to attend AA meetings on a regular basis to feel connected and avoid the pitfalls of isolation. Staying plugged in to the solution is imperative for me. I also stay diligent with prayer and meditation to keep myself focused and on track. My happiness is directly correlated to how connected I am to God. We'll never reach our goals without becoming consistent in our habits. Success is the natural result of consistent habits.

I am so grateful to be back on track. My sobriety is so much more than not drinking. What I really have is a daily reprieve contingent on the maintenance of my spiritual condition. When I got tangled up emotionally, my spiritual condition suffered greatly. When a recovering alcoholic loses serenity, sobriety is usually next. I'm grateful I didn't return to drinking, but if I stayed as miserable as I'd become, there's no telling what could have happened. I took my sobriety for granted, and I paid dearly for it. When this happens, the first step is recognizing our complacency and the next step is doing something about it. It's all about surrender. The first surrender is admitting we are powerless over alcohol. The second surrender is giving up control and trusting in the will of God. Believing and knowing that God loves me more than I could ever love myself creates blind trust. This trust allows me to live with confidence and security. God is consistent, and so is His love. I am a childish alcoholic, and I believe

God uses unpleasant circumstances to help me grow up. God wants to strengthen, sharpen, and transform us into something greater. When I trust God during tough times, I don't need to understand why things happen the way they do. God uses messy situations to draw us closer to Him, awaken our need for Him, and shape our character.

To get God's power, give Him your trust. This trust gives me the strength to enjoy my life, just as it will for you. It is such an inexplicable gift to feel God's love in my heart again. Emotional sobriety allows me to be good to other people and let love flow in and out of me all day. Emotional sobriety takes time, patience, and dedication to maintain, but you can share in the full abundance of this gift as well. Our job is to stay spiritually fit through love, forgiveness, acceptance, gratitude, and obedience.

Made in the USA
Columbia, SC
22 September 2019